French Knot Pictures

CHRISTINE HARRIS

MILNER CRAFT SERIES

French Knot Pictures

Christine Harris

SALLY MILNER PUBLISHING

To my Mother, Dorothy Ellen Miller

First published in 1994 by
Sally Milner Publishing Pty Ltd
PO Box 2104
Bowral NSW 2576
Australia

Reprinted 1995(twice),1999, 2000

© Christine Harris 1994
Design and typesetting by Shirley Peters
Photography by Benjamin Huie
Illustrations by Don Bradford
Printed in Australia by Impact Printing

The project 'The Pergola', featured in the colour
pages, was reproduced from a photograph of the
original watercolour by Lilian Stannard (1877-1944),
*An Old Paved Walk in a Hertfordshire Garden:
'The Pergola'*. Signed. $9^{3}/_{4}$" x $13^{1}/_{2}$", by courtesy
of Fine-Lines Fine Art, of Shipston-on-Stour,
Warwickshire, England.

National Library of Australia
Cataloguing-in-Publication data:
Harris, Christine, 1947–
French knot pictures

ISBN 1 86351 235 7

1.Embroidery. 2. Embroidery – Patterns. I. Title.
(Series : Milner craft series).
746.44042

Acknowledgements

I thank Dolfus-Mieg and Cie, Paris, for donating threads and for granting permission to use the DMC© trademark throughout this book.

I would like to thank Vickie Clark for her contribution to the typing of this manuscript. Also my mother, Dorothy Miller, for her contribution to the typing — it was a task shared.

Other contributors who I wish to thank are:

Don Bradford, for his excellent illustrations. Jane Courtenay for the use of her scene. Friends and students who have offered such encouragement and had such a long wait for this book.

Christine Harris 1994

Contents

Introduction   6

Materials   7

  Threads   7

  Fabrics   9

  Needles   9

Techniques   10

  Transferring the design 10

  Enlarging or reducing a design 10

  Care and laundering   11

  Points to remember   11

  General notes   13

  Finding a picture to work from 13

  Scenes in French knots   14

Projects   15

  The parterre garden   15

  Herbaceous borders   19

  The garden path   28

  A pram in the garden   34

  The pergola   37

  The blossom tree   45

  Lingerie bag   52

  Pot pourri stem   54

  Vase of flowers   55

  Brooch   58

Introduction

I was first introduced to the French knot about ten years ago and it is one of my favourite stitches because of its versatility. My first effort was quite ordinary, although I thoroughly enjoyed the project at the time.

However, I decided that I could improve on what I had done and decided to explore the endless possibilities that I saw awaiting me. The technique that I use gradually evolved through trial and error over several projects. I feel that the scenes produced in this book really are needle art. It is amazing to think that such depth and perspective can be achieved with the use of just one stitch — the French knot.

My aim in writing this book is, hopefully, to inspire you to explore scenes beyond those given in this text so that you will create your own masterpieces and derive as much pleasure and satisfaction as I have from this form of embroidery.

Materials

THREADS

To simplify the given projects for the purposes of this book, I have used DMC stranded cotton and incorporated a little silk ribbon or silk thread occasionally as a highlight. However, when you embark on projects of your own, you should include a far greater variety of threads – all work well and some wonderful effects can be achieved. Be adventurous. If using stranded cotton, you can use from one to the full six strands, depending on the size knot you need.

DMC Perle 5 and Perle 8 can be incorporated. I have used Perle 5 with a single strand of stranded cotton to give just a hint of another colour. Do not be afraid to mix threads as well as colours. Two different threads worked together in the one needle can create just the effect you are looking for.

There are many beautiful silk threads on the market today, ranging from a matt finish to a high lustre. These are all fun to work with and all are suitable for French knot embroidery. Those with a high lustre can be used to create interesting highlights when scattered through a particular section of your work.

Silk ribbon is also a favourite of mine. I generally use 2 mm (1/16") but if I have only 4 mm (3/16") in the colour that I need, I use a fine needle and pull the knot very tight. I don't usually work whole areas with silk ribbon but tend to use it as a highlight.

Some of my students have incorporated Balgar blending filaments, and others have used some tiny beads, which create an interesting effect and look wonderful.

Once again I emphasise the point, don't hesitate to try something a little different. You should derive so much pleasure and satisfaction from achieving something that is uniquely yours.

Feel free to use whatever threads you have at your disposal. Part of the joy of this form of embroidery is using a bit of this and a bit of that – it's great fun. If, however, you do not have a wide variety of thread types in your sewing basket, you can achieve some striking effects just with stranded cottons used on their own.

Generally, you need only very small quantities of a given colour, so look at some of the threads that may be left over from kits, or other completed projects. These leftover threads can be so useful when only a touch of a required shade is needed. Remember that you can achieve subtle shading, or a more dramatic effect, by using two or more colours in the needle together.

Use only short lengths of threads. Because you are working small areas, you require only small amounts of any given colour or combination of colours. A thread length of 20 cm (8") is sufficient. Do not be tempted to use longer lengths as the thread wears and frays.

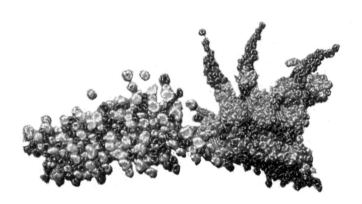

FABRICS

For the scenes worked entirely in French knots, I use only calico, although homespun works well too. Many of my students have suggested using a very fine linen. Linens, however, even the fine closely woven ones, are not suitable. If you are using a single strand of thread, with a size 10 needle, the tiny knots pull through. For this reason, a closely woven fabric such as calico is the obvious choice. The fabric is going to be completely covered, none of the base fabric will be exposed, so the appearance of the base fabric is not important.

Before you begin your embroidery, I suggest that you launder the calico to remove any dressing from the fabric. For small projects, such as pot pourri bags or lingerie bags, silk, satin or taffeta are suitable.

NEEDLES

There are no definite rules regarding which needle to use. For French knot embroidery, I recommend crewel needles for most of the work. Crewel needles have a sharp point and a long eye, which makes them easy to thread.

If using a single strand of embroidery thread, I always use a size 10 crewel needle. However, some embroiderers find this fine needle difficult to thread so I tell my students to use the finest needle that they can thread. The only rule that I follow is, always use the finest needle that will accommodate the thread or threads in use. This will give you firm knots which are tidy. If you use a larger needle than required, your knots will be loopy and will not sit well. Your work will then take on an entirely different appearance.

If I find it difficult to thread a crewel needle when using a heavier thread, I use a straw needle.

The choice of which type of needle to use is entirely personal preference.

Techniques

TRANSFERRING THE DESIGN

A 2B lead pencil with a sharp point is ideal to trace the design directly onto the fabric. This will wash out easily when embroidery has been completed.

If you have access to a light box, you can trace the design easily.

Alternatively, you can improvise a light source in one of two ways: either with a lamp under a glass coffee table, or by taping the design onto a window then placing the fabric over this so that the sun is your light source.

For the designs in this book you can mark in all of the details. However, if you are working from a picture of your own, it is not necessary to mark in every detail.

ENLARGING OR REDUCING THE DESIGN

When you are choosing a scene to embroider, the size of your chosen scene is not important. You can enlarge or reduce the size of the original to suit your requirements. This can be done on a photocopier. If you do not have access to a photocopier, you can alter the size of your design by using a grid system.

Draw a grid over your chosen scene. If, for example, this scene measured 19 cm x 13 cm (7½" x 5") you would draw a box around the outside. Draw two evenly spaced lines on the short side of the picture so that it is evenly divided into three sections. Then draw three evenly spaced lines on the long side of the picture so that it is evenly divided into four sections.

Draw a second grid the size you want your picture to be, perhaps, for example, 8.5 cm x 6.5 cm (3½" x 2½"). This reduced grid should have the same number of lines as the first. The next step is to draw the design onto your second grid. Begin by finding a focal point on the large picture and, with a sharp lead pencil, draw this feature onto the reduced grid. If, for example, you have a tree trunk in one square of the large grid, begin by drawing this in the corresponding square on the smaller grid. Mark in the major features of the picture. It is not necessary to draw in every detail as this becomes tedious and confusing.

As you work, you may find it necessary to mark in additional areas as a guide. Some of the finer details will be omitted. This system works in exactly the same way if you have a small picture and wish to enlarge it.

CARE AND LAUNDERING

I like to wash my embroideries before they are framed. Gentle hand washing in warm, soapy water using pure soap is recommended. Rinse thoroughly to remove all traces of soap. Do not wring the fabric, but allow it to drip dry. Place the damp embroidery right side down to press. As the knots are massed closely together, heavy pressing is not necessary. Hold a steam iron just above the embroidery and gently steam. Press the fabric surrounding your embroidered picture.

POINTS TO REMEMBER

- Shading is achieved by combining different coloured threads worked together in the one needle.
- Depth, dimension and perspective are achieved by varying the size of the knot. Knots vary in size from very small, e.g. one strand of thread using a size 9 or 10 crewel needle, to large knots using six strands of thread, or heavier threads such as Perle 5 or silk ribbon.
- If working a scene, for example a garden, cluster the knots very closely together in the garden area. If working the sky, a path or a grassed area, do not work the knots as closely together. This helps achieve depth and dimension.

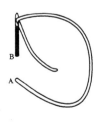

Straight Stitch

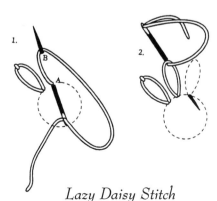

Lazy Daisy Stitch

Couching

- If the instructions say to work a colour over a base colour, this means work one layer of knots closely together and then work another layer of knots over the first. This is done for two reasons. First, it can achieve shading and secondly, it may be used to achieve depth.
- Always use the smallest needle that will accommodate the thread in use. This achieves very firm knots.
- Remember to combine colours and/or threads worked together. For example, if you are trying to represent large white flowers with a blue centre, you could use Perle 5 with a single strand of blue stranded cotton. This will give just a hint of colour through the flowers.
- When working French knots, be careful not to take the needle back through the same hole that you brought your needle up. Always take the needle a little out from this original hole. If you do not do this your knot will be pulled through to the back of the work.
- When the instructions refer to knots, it always means French knots. Use only French knots. Do not be tempted to use colonial knots. If a larger knot is required, use a heavier thread.
- When the instructions say to use one colour together with another colour, e.g. one each of 340 and 3727, it means that these colours are worked together in the one needle.
- Always use an embroidery hoop to keep the fabric taut. This will help you develop a rhythm. The small plastic hoops are comfortable to use. If, however, you choose the traditional wooden embroidery hoop, remember to bind the inner ring with white cotton tape.
- When the instructions say to fill the area, it always means fill the area with French knots.
- Do not use long lengths of thread. A maximum length of 30 cm (12") is ideal.
- Keep a pin cushion in your work basket with several needles threaded with colours that are used frequently.
- Read through all of the instructions before beginning a project.
- You can begin with a knot in your thread.

GENERAL NOTES

For French knot embroidery, the only stitches that I use are French knots, with an occasional straight stitch to emphasise a particular feature. Many students ask, 'Why not use colonial knots?' The choice is one of personal preference for me as I enjoy working in French knots. If I need a larger knot, I simply increase the number of threads, or the type of thread. This varying of the size of the knots with the different weights of thread is how I achieve depth, dimension and perspective.

I very rarely work an area using a single colour as this tends to look very flat. For your picture to come to life you need to introduce shading. It need only be very subtle but it will make such a difference to the finished picture.

When working a picture of your own choosing, look carefully at the picture. Begin your work at a main focal point and work out from this point, completing each feature as you work out from this area. Do not start in one corner and then jump to an entirely different section of the picture and hope that all the pieces will join up as this will create problems. If you work out from a given point you will find it easier to achieve perspective and depth.

When working a garden scene, there may be a bed of roses or daffodils. Bear in mind that you will not get a rose to look like a rose, nor a daffodil to look like a daffodil — your French knot flowers will be a representation of the original. Once you are comfortable with this concept your garden will blossom straight from the needle.

FINDING A PICTURE TO WORK FROM

There are many sources of inspiration for French knot embroidery, particularly for the scenes in French knots. One book that I recommend is *Victorian Flower Gardens* by Andrew Clayton-Payne. This book features nineteenth-century watercolours. When you look into the pictures the shading is ideal and a wonderful guide for the embroiderer.

On the market today there are many beautiful greeting cards available. Many of the pictures featured on these cards can be used as a guide to create a French knot picture. Many of Monet's works are featured on cards and his gardens are ideal to work in French knots.

When choosing a picture to work from, most students find it more helpful to choose an actual work by an artist rather than a picture from a magazine, book or a drawing of their own. If working from a painting, particularly a watercolour, the artist has provided the embroiderer with a guide to the shading. You have to look into the painting to appreciate the shading within. Pictures taken from books and magazines, although often pretty, do not, on close examination, offer the same degree of subtle colour change that is found in a painting. Some students are happy to work from these, while the majority find it easier to work from a painting where the guide to colour change is more definite.

When choosing a picture to work from, the most important point to remember is to choose something that really appeals to you. The size does not matter as it can be enlarged or reduced (see *Enlarging or reducing the design*, page 10). The picture may be a cottage garden, landscape, seascape or still life. Pictures can also be simplified by omitting some of the detail, so do not be overwhelmed if your chosen picture has a great deal of detail.

THE FRENCH KNOT

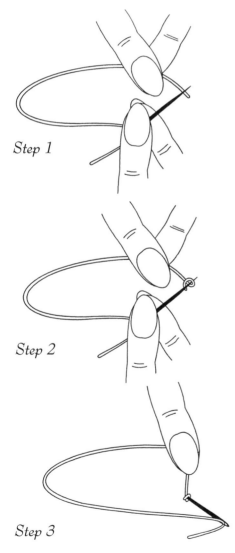

Step 1

Step 2

Step 3

SCENES IN FRENCH KNOTS

These scenes are all worked in miniature. I recommend that when you work scenes of your own choice that you do not exceed a maximum size of 5 cm x 7 cm (3" x 2"). There are two significant reasons for this recommendation. First, I feel that the charm of these little pictures lies in their size. If you work a larger picture, it becomes increasingly difficult to achieve the depth and dimension. Secondly, there is a significant time factor involved. A picture of the recommended size will take approximately 15 hours to complete.

There are large numbers of colours required for these scenes, the variety of colours being necessary to achieve the shading. Many of the colours used require only very small quantities of thread so you may wish to substitute some of the suggested colours with ones that you already have rather than purchase the additional threads. If you choose to alter the colour scheme, the completed picture will, of course, take on a quite different appearance.

I shall emphasise once again that you must, at all times, use the finest needle that will accommodate the thread in use. These scenes are masses upon masses of very firm knots.

The Parterre Garden

Herbaceous Border

The Garden Path

A Pram in the Garden

Projects

The Parterre Garden

Parterre gardens are generally associated with palaces or grand villas and developed from the formal knot garden which was popular during mediaeval times. Royal knot gardens were decorated with carved wooden beasts. Parterre gardens can be seen on a grand scale in England, at Hampton Court and Hall's Crofts, Stratford-on-Avon. In the USA, the gardens of Virginia, particularly those at Williamsburg, are full of parterres.

This design is based on a garden plan. It is easy, very effective and fun to do.

FABRIC REQUIRED:

20 cm (8") square piece of calico

THREADS REQUIRED:

Waterlilies by Caron. Colour Gobi Sand
Marlitt, white, optional or DMC blanc neige
Balger blending filament. Silver 001
1m (1 yd) x 2 mm (1/16") buttercup yellow silk ribbon

DMC stranded cotton (floss)

471 avocado green, very light	934 black avocado green
523 fern green, light	966 baby green, medium
726 topaz, light	3346 hunter green
745 yellow, light	3347 yellow green, medium
758 pale terracotta, very light	blanc neige, white

ADDITIONAL REQUIREMENTS:

A small embroidery hoop
A variety of needles

METHOD:

1. Using two strands of Marlitt with an equal length of blending filament, work 25–30 knots scattered through the area. If you choose not to use the Marlitt, substitute three strands of DMC blanc neige.
   With two strands of 966, work approximately 25 knots scattered between the white already worked.
   Using a single strand of 934, fill any remaining un-worked area. Do not work the outer edges of this

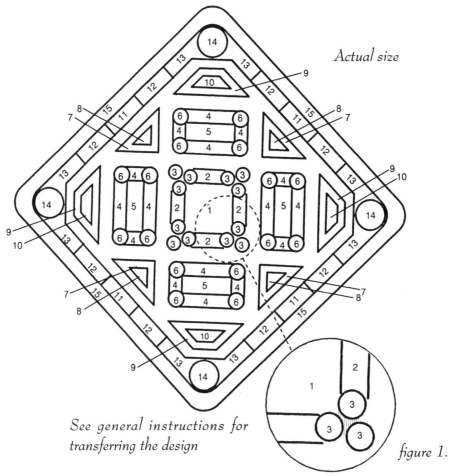

Actual size

See general instructions for transferring the design

figure 1.

setion as an even straight line — leave a few small spaces which will be filled with the next colour used.

At each corner of this section there are three circles. Use a single strand of 934 to define the area between these circles. See figure 1.

2. Using a single strand of 966, fill a little less than half the area with knots.

   Then, with a single strand of blanc neige, fill the remaining unworked area with knots worked closely together.

3. With a single strand of 3346, fill all of the circles. Work a few extra knots on top of base layer to give a rounded appearance.

4. Take a single strand of 934 and work a broken line of knots between this garden bed and all adjoining paved areas. This will give a sharp definition of the flower beds. Using a single strand of 471, fill these areas with

closely worked knots. With a single strand of 745 and then 758, work some knots on top of the base layer so that the flowers are sitting on the greenery.

Take a single strand of Waterlilies Gobi Sand and fill all of the paved area, that is, all areas between the numbered garden beds.

5. Using a single strand of 934, work a row of knots along the inside edge of section 4. Scatter about six clusters of three knots through this area.

   Using two strands of 966, scatter approximately 10–12 knots through this area between those already worked.

   With 2 mm (¹⁄₁₆″) buttercup yellow silk ribbon, scatter about seven knots through the area.

   Using two strands of 745, fill any remaining unworked areas.

6. Take a single strand of 3346 and fill the circles with closely worked knots. Work some knots on top of the base layer to give a rounded appearance.

7. With a single strand of 523, fill the area with very closely worked knots.

   Using a single strand of blanc neige, scatter some knots on top of the green base layer.

8. Take a single strand of 3346 and fill this area. Using two strands of 745, work five or six knots on top of the green base layer.

9. Using a single strand of 3347, fill this area.

10. With a single strand of blanc neige, work a line of knots joining section 9 so that this area is outlined in white. Scatter a few knots through the area.

    Using a single strand of 3346, fill the remaining area.

11. With two strands of 745 together with one strand of 726, work about 10–12 knots scattered through the area.

    Using two strands of 966, fill most of the remaining area leaving just enough room to work a single line of knots along both edges.

12. Using two strands of blanc neige, work about seven knots in this section.

    Using two strands of 966, fill most of the remaining area, but once again leave enough room to work a single line of knots along both edges.

13. Work as for 11, but work less of lemon, approximately five knots.

    Once sections 11, 12 and 13 have been completed, use a single strand of 934 to work a single row of knots along both edges of these areas. Any small, unworked spaces can be filled with this colour. Continue the line of knots, working right around the edge of 14 to define this garden bed.

14. Using two strands of 3346, fill the circles. When completed, use a single strand of blanc neige to scatter some flowers on top of the base layer.

15. With a single strand of 3347, fill the area.

    You may wish to work your initials and the date in this area. It can be worked either in French knots or a single thread couched on top of the knots.

Herbaceous Borders

This is a very pretty picture. There is a lot of detail but your patience shall be rewarded — it is well worth the effort.

FABRIC REQUIRED:

> 20 cm (8") square piece of calico

THREADS REQUIRED:

> DMC stranded cotton (floss)

Ecru	3013 olive green, pale
Blanc neige, white	3022 brown grey, medium
210 lavender	3023 brown grey, light
211 lavender, light	3041 antique violet, pale
221 shell pink, dark	3042 antique violet
340 blue violet	3053 green grey
341 blue violet, light	3348 yellow green, light
351 peach, very dark	3362 pine green, dark
352 peach, dark	3363 pine green, medium
503 blue green, medium	3364 pine green
504 blue green, light	3688 rose pink
676 old gold, light	3713 salmon, very light
727 topaz, very light	3727 pink mauve
730 olive green, very dark	3731 dusty rose, very dark
738 caramel, light	3743 antique violet, very pale
739 tan, very light	3753 antique blue, very light
761 pearl grey	3756 baby blue, very light
778 antique mauve, very light	3772 negro flesh
927 grey green	3773 sportsman flesh, medium
950 salmon pink	3774 sportsman flesh, very light

ADDITIONAL REQUIREMENTS:

> A small embroidery hoop
> A variety of needles of various sizes

METHOD:

> 1. Using three strands of ecru together with one strand of 3727, work clusters of knots leaving some spaces between the clusters to fill with green.
> Take two strands of ecru and work some more knots around and between those already worked, so that the knots in the clusters are now massed very closely

Actual size

See general instructions for transferring the design

together, but still leaving small spaces between the clusters.

Using a single strand of 3362, scatter small knots around the clusters of flowers. Then use a single strand of 3363 to fill any unworked areas.

With a single strand of 3362, scatter some knots around the outline of those flowers at the top of this section. The knots should be worked very close to the flowers.

2. With two strands of 778, scatter about 15 knots through the area.

Using a single thread of 3364, fill about half the remaining area with knots and then with a single strand of 503, fill the remaining area. Finally, work several small, straight stitches on top of the green to represent stems.

3. Using one strand of 778 together with one strand of 3727, fill the area with knots.

With a single strand of 3362, work some small knots between those already worked.

4. Using a single strand of 3362, work lines of knots where indicated.

Using a single strand of 3041, fill the remaining area. Scatter about six knots on top of those already worked and then a few very small straight stitches fanning out from the bottom towards the top.

5. Using a single strand of 3348, work knots more

densely at the top of this area, thinning out the number of knots as you work toward the bottom of the picture.

With a single strand of 3363, fill in the remaining area.

Then with a single strand of 3348, work some very small straight stitches scattered on top of the knots.

6. Using a single strand of 3363, outline the tree with knots, then fill about half the area with knots.

Fill the remaining spaces with a single strand of 730 and then work several more knots, using 3363 on top of those already worked.

Using a single strand of 3363, work several very small straight stitches in an up–down direction.

7. Take a single strand of 730 and fill most of the area.

Using a single strand of 3363, scatter some knots throughout the area, then with a single strand of 730, work a few very small stitches in an up-down direction.

8. Using three strands of 351 together with two strands of 352, work seven knots, four within this area and three scattered beyond this point.

Using three strands of 351, work about six or seven knots between those already worked. If you have a small space in section 2, you may like to work one or two knots in this colour in this section.

Using a single strand of 3362 fill about half of the area with knots.

Take a single strand of 3363 and fill the remaining area.

With a single strand of 3363, work some straight stitches to represent stems coming from the flowers to the bottom of the picture.

9. Using a single strand of 3042, fill about half of the area and then take a single strand of 3743 and fill the remaining area.

10. Using a single strand of 3743, and beginning at the bottom of the picture, half fill the lower half of this area with knots.

With a single strand of 504, fill most of the remaining area, except for the top of this section.

Using a single strand of 503, scatter knots between

those already worked.

Take a single strand of 503 and fill any remaining areas at the top of this section.

Using a single strand of 3363, work some straight stitch stems for the flowers in the direction of section 8.

11. Using two strands of ecru, fill about half the area, concentrating all of these knots in the top of this section. Then scatter a few single strand knots of this colour through the knots already worked.

    With single strands each of 3363 and 503, fill the remaining area.

12. Using two strands of 778 together with one strand of 221, work knots fairly closely together at the top of this area so that approximately half of this area is filled.

    With a single strand of 927, fill the remaining area, then work a few very short straight stitches on top of the knots.

13. With one strand of 223 together with one strand of 224, work clusters of three knots worked closely together, scattered through the area.

    Using a single strand of 224, work more knots around and on top of the clusters already worked. Leave a little space between the clusters of knots.

    Using a single strand of 3362 with an occasional single strand of 3363, fill the remaining spaces.

    With a single strand of 3362, work a few tiny stitches on top of the green knots to represent stems.

14. Using a single strand of 3713, fill most of the area, then work more knots on top of those already worked.

    Using a single strand of 3363, work some green knots in any remaining spaces.

15. Take a single strand of 341 and fill the shaded area with a single layer of knots. Work a few knots on top of those worked so that you have a second layer.

    Using a single strand of 340, fill the remaining area with a single layer of knots.

15a. Take a single strand of 3363 and fill the area.

16. Using a single strand of 3713, fill the area. With a single strand of 3363, work five or six knots at the base of these flowers.

17. Using a single strand of 727 and then 676, work about equal numbers of knots in these two colours in the top half of this section.

    Take a single strand of 3053 and fill the remaining area.

18. Using a single strand of 340, fill the area.

19. With a single strand of 761, fill most of the area and then with a single strand of 3363, fill the remaining area.

20. Using a single strand of blanc neige, fill the area.

    Using a single strand of 3362, work some knots along the base of sections 11, 12, 13, 16 and 20. Small knots worked at random along the bottom of this garden will help define the area.

21. Using a single strand of 3743, half fill the lower half of this section. Using a single strand of 3348, fill the remaining spaces in this lower half with knots.

    With a single strand of 3348, scatter some knots through this section.

    Using a single strand of 504, fill any remaining spaces.

22. Using a single strand of each colour, fill this section with equal numbers of 3348, 3743 and 503.

    Then with a single strand of 730, work one long straight stitch from the lower corner of section 21, ending at section 11, so that the grassed area of 21 is defined. Then work another long straight stitch from above 11 to the upper end of 22. Work straight stitches along the edge of 10, ending at the edge of section 9.

23. *The Path:* The knots filling the path are not massed tightly together, but worked a little more sparsely than the previous embroidery.

    Using a single strand of 3743, fill approximately half of the area. Then take a single strand of 739 to fill any remaining area.

24. Using single strands of 739 and then ecru, fill the area.

    Using two strands of 352, scatter five single knots across the bottom of the path to represent fallen petals.

25. With a single strand of 504, work one row of knots along the lower edge of this section, with an occasional

knot scattered above to form a broken second row.

Using a single strand of blanc neige, fill the remaining area.

With a single strand of 730, work some short straight stitches from left to right across the bottom of this section. These small stitches will define the grassed area from the path.

26. Using a single strand of blanc neige, fill the area.

27. Take two strands of 351 and work three or four knots in the lower part of this section. Then using a single strand of the same colour, scatter another four or five knots.

    Using a single strand of 3363 and then 503, fill the remaining area.

28. With a single strand of 504, fill the area.

29. With a single strand of 761, fill the area.

30. Using a single strand of 3688 and then 3363, fill the area.

31. As for 15.

32. Using a single strand of 727 and then 676, fill the area. Work a few knots on top of those already worked to form a second layer.

    Just along the top of sections 26 and 29, scatter a few single strand knots using 503, 3363 and 727.

33. With a single strand of blanc neige, fill most of the area then, using a single strand of 3363, work about three or four very short straight stitches between the knots.

    Using a single strand of 503, work four or five knots on the right-hand side of this area, next to the white knots.

34. Using a single strand of 3713, work knots so that they are in more or less horizontal rows, then with single strands each of 503, 3363 and 3053, fill the remaining area.

35. With a single strand of 3772, work the straight stitches, as illustrated, to represent the brick work.

    Using a single strand of 950, work knots between the straight stitches.

36. As for 35.

37. Take a single strand of 3713 and fill most of the area.

Work several more knots on top to form a second layer. With a single strand of 3053, work some knots between the pink, concentrating on the right-hand side.

38. Using two strands of 3731, work the knots closely together in the lower part of this section, spacing them a little further apart toward the top.

   With a single strand of the same colour, fill in any spaces and work a few knots at the sides of the larger knots. The top of this flower should consist of two or three single-strand knots.

39. Using three strands, then two strands of 3731, work as for 38.

40. With a single strand each of 210 and 211, fill the area. Work a second layer on top of the first layer so that the knots are very closely massed together.

   Using a single strand of 3363, scatter an occasional knot through the spray, then work more green knots around the outside edge of this section.

41. Using four strands of ecru, work about six or eight knots towards the bottom of this section. Reduce from four strands to three strands and work about the same number of knots a little higher. Reduce to two strands and scatter more knots in the upper part of this section.

   Take three strands of 3053 and scatter knots throughout the area.

   Using two strands of 3348, scatter more knots so that the entire area is almost filled, then with a single strand of 730, fill any small spaces.

   Should there be any small spaces left along the left-hand edge of the picture, fill these spaces with a single strand of 950.

   Across the top of sections 35 and 36, there is a single straight stitch.

   Using a single strand of 3774, work a single horizontal row of knots along the outer edge of this straight stitch.

42. With a single strand of each of 3772, 3773, 224 and 738, work equal numbers of knots in each colour. In the centre of the tree, mass the knots closely together

but do not have them worked closely together toward the outside edge. Leave a few small spaces to be filled in with the colour to be used for the sky or the adjoining trees.

43. Using a single strand of 3743, fill the area on the right-hand side of this section. Work the knots closely together in the lower part of this section but leave some spaces toward the top of the section.

    Take a single strand of 3756 and fill the unworked spaces in the top of the tree.

    Using a single strand each of 3743 and then 3023, fill the remaining area with equal numbers of each colour.

44. With a single strand of 730, work the straight stitches where indicated.

    Using a single strand of 3023 and beginning at the top of the tree, work the outline of the tree and small clusters of knots, leaving small areas unworked. As you work down the tree, introduce 3022. The middle section of the tree is made up of equal numbers of 3022 and 3023, but still leaving a few small spaces unworked. At the bottom section of the tree, work clusters of single-strand 730. These clusters should consist of two to four knots. Fill any remaining spaces with 3022.

45. Using a single strand of 3013, fill about half the area.

    Then with a single strand of 3023, fill the remaining spaces at the bottom of the tree. As you work towards the top of the tree, leave an occasional space.

46. Take a single strand of 3023 and work knots in the lower part this section. Scatter a few knots of this colour throughout the remaining area.

    Using a single strand of 3743, fill the remaining area.

47. Using a single strand of 3743, fill a little less than half of the area with knots.

    With a single strand of 504, fill the remaining area.

48. Using a single strand of 3023, fill the area.

49. Using a single strand of 3042, fill the area.

50. *The Sky:* The knots filling the sky are not massed tightly together but worked a little more sparsely than the other embroidery.

    Using a single strand of 341, scatter some knots in the

shaded area in the top right-hand corner, thinning the number of knots of this colour as you work towards the centre of the picture.

Using a single strand of 3756 in the dotted area, scatter knots sparsely.

With a single strand of 3753, fill the remaining area of the sky and then with a single strand of 3756, fill any unworked areas in 45.

You can work your initials and the year with a single strand of ecru or blanc neige in the lower left-hand corner if desired.

The Garden Path

FABRIC REQUIRED:

20 cm (8") square piece of calico

THREADS REQUIRED:

DMC stranded cotton (floss)

Blanc neige – white	746 off white
211 lavender, light	754 peach flesh, light
315 antique mauve, very dark	760 salmon
340 blue violet	775 baby blue, very light
341 blue violet, light	783 topaz, medium
352 coral, light	800 sky blue
353 peach flesh	833 golden olive, light
470 avocado, light	834 golden olive, very light
502 blue green	841 beige brown, light
504 blue green, light	927 grey green, light
523 fern green, light	3013 khaki green, light
554 violet, light	3041 antique violet, medium
604 cranberry	3042 antique violet, light
605 cranberry, very light	3362 pine green, dark
712 cream	3687 mauve
727 topaz, very light	3689 mauve, light
732 olive green	3743 antique violet, very light
733 olive green, medium	A brown of your choice to be used
738 tan, very light	on the house

ADDITIONAL REQUIREMENTS:

A small hoop
A variety of needles of various sizes

METHOD

1. Using three strands of 746, scatter seven or eight knots evenly spaced through this area.
   Fill the remaining area with single-strand knots, using 504 and 927, with approximately the same number of knots of each colour. When the area has been completely filled with knots, use a single strand of 927 to work short straight stitches over the green area. Work these straight stitches parallel to the path.

2. Work the shaded area with 3 strands, 2 of 760 with one of 353.

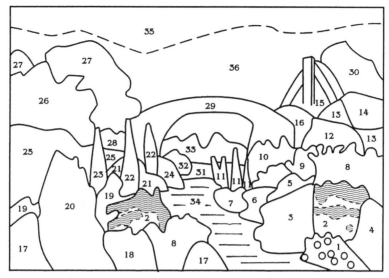

See general instructions for transferring the design

Actual size

Fill the remaining area with knots, using a single strand of 523 with a very occasional 3362.

When the area has been filled with green, work a few vertical straight stitches in a single strand of 523 over the knots. Between areas 2 and 3, work a few single-strand knots in 523.

3. This section is worked with two different colour combinations using three strands — two strands of blanc neige with one strand 341 and then 2 strands of 341 with one strand of white. Fill the upper section with these combinations.

   Leave the lower section of this area to fill with a single strand of 523 with an occasional 3362.

4. Using two strands, one of 783 together with one of

315, scatter eight to ten knots through the area. Remove the 315, then work more knots in the two strands of 783 so that most of the area is filled. Fill any gaps with green 523.

5. Using two strands, one each of 760 and 353, fill the area. Work about three or four knots over the base layer to give some dimension.
Between areas 3 and 5, work a single row in a single strand of 523.

6. Using three strands of 727, work about five knots, then reduce to two strands and work about five or six knots. Fill any gaps with a single strand of 470.

7. Scatter approximately ten knots using two strands of 783. Fill the remaining area with a single strand of 523.

8. Using two strands of white together with one strand of 315, scatter knots towards the top of this area. Remove one of the white threads, leaving one white together with one 315. Scatter a number of knots using this combination in the same area. Then, using three strands of white, scatter a few more knots so that the upper area is completely covered. Fill in the remaining lower section of this area with a single strand of 3013. Work a few straight stitches over the green knots wherever they will fit.

9. Using two strands of 727, together with one strand of 783, scatter six or seven knots through the area. Fill the remaining area with single-strand 3013. Work a few vertical straight stitches on the green.

10. With a single strand of 605 and then 604, work about equal numbers of knots in these two colours in the upper section of this area. Work several knots in either pink over the base layer of knots. Leave a small area along the lower edge of this section. Fill this lower section with single-strand 523.

11. Using a single strand of 340, fill the area and then work extra knots over these at the base of the flowers.

12. Using one strand of 732, together with one of 733, scatter about six knots in this area. Pull the knots tightly so that they are small. Fill the remaining area with equal numbers of single strands of 733 and 833.

'The Pergola'

Original water-colour painting by
Lilian Stannard

The Blossom Tree

Vase of Flowers

Brooch

Framed picture, Vase of Flowers Box,
Brooch, Pot Pourri Stem, and
Lingerie Bag

My work bench

13. Using single strands of 833 and then 3042, fill the area with equal numbers of these colours.

14. Using a single strand of 523 and then 502, fill this area with equal numbers of these colours.

15. *The House:* All worked in a single strand.

    Left-hand Gable: Work a single row of knots in 841 in a straight line to outline the roof. Then work two or three knots sitting above those already worked. Fill the spaces in this second row with 3042 so that you have two rows sitting very closely together. The first row consists of all 841, while the second row has two or three knots of 841 and the remaining knots are 3042.

    Right-hand Gable: Work a single row of knots in 841 to outline the area which defines the roof from the house. Work about three knots along this line in a dark brown of your choice.

    Chimney: Outline with 841, with an occasional dark brown (as used on the gable) on the right-hand side of the chimney.

    Roof: Work in 3042.

    Fill the remaining house and centre of the chimney with 738.

16. Using single strands, fill the area predominantly with 523, with some 470 scattered through the area.

17. Using a single strand of 502, fill the area. Work about four to six knots, using two strands of 504 on top of the base colour — or this section may be used to work your initials and the date as I have done.

18. Using two strands of 504, together with one strand of 712, fill a little more than half the area. Leave a little room in the lower section of this area to work some green. Using two strands of 712 anywhere that there may be any gaps, work a few knots on top of this base layer. Fill the remaining unworked area with a single-strand 502 and work a few vertical straight stitches over the knots.

19. Using a single strand of 211, fill the centre area. When the base colour has been completed, work another layer of knots (but don't work them as closely together as the base layer) over the first using 554. Using a single strand of 502, work a row of knots

between areas 2 and 19. This will give better definition of colour.

20. With six strands of 3689, work some knots in the lower section of this area. Reduce to three strands of 3689 and continue to scatter knots through the upper section of this area. Using two strands of 523, together with one strand of 504, scatter knots between the pink already worked. Any small spaces that are remaining fill with a single strand of 504.

21. Using one strand of 341 together with one strand of white, fill the area. Then work about four to six knots, in a single strand of 341, on top of the base colour. Work a few knots using a single strand of 502 above and below this area to define the area.

22. *The larger flower on the left-hand side:* Fill the lower section with three strands of 3687, then reduce to two strands and complete the upper section of the flower. Using two strands of 502, work an occasional knot through the flower and along the sides to represent leaves.

    The smaller flower on the right-hand side: Using two strands of 3687 for the lower section of the flower, reduce to a single strand of 3687 to complete the upper section of the flower. Then using a single strand of 502, work an occasional knot on either side to represent leaves.

23. Work as for the larger flower in 22, but use white.

24. Using a single strand of 341, fill the entire area, then work about four to six knots in a single strand of 340 on top of the base colour.

25. Work as for number 12, but scatter a few single strands of 738. When the area has been filled, work a number of scattered small straight stitches to represent branches, using single-strand 738.

26. Using single strands, scatter equal numbers of 738 and 834.

27. All worked in single strand. Using 834, scatter about 12–15 knots. Using 738, work scattered knots around the outline of the tree. Using 775, scatter about 12 knots near the outline of the tree. Using 3042, scatter about 24 knots through the area. Using 3041, fill in

any remaining gaps.

28. With single strands, fill the area with equal numbers of 3041 and 3042.

29. With single strands, fill the area with equal numbers of 754, 712, 3013, 353 and 352.

30. Using single strands, outline area with 3041 then fill the area with equal numbers of 3041 and 502, with an occasional 775.

31. Using a single strand of 504, fill the area.

32. Using a single strand of 605, fill the area.

33. Using a single strand, fill the area with 3042.

34. *Path:* All worked in a single strand.

   Along the right-hand edge, between the path and the garden, work an occasional 3362. Between the path and area 31, work some very short straight stitches of 502. For the horizontal lines on the path, work a row of 3743 where these lines are.

   Fill the remaining path area with 738 and with an occasional 754.

35. Using single strand of 800, scatter an occasional knot.

36. Using a single strand of 775, fill the remaining area.

A Pram in the Garden

This picture would make a special gift for a new baby. It would look delightful framed, or perhaps made into a cushion.

FABRIC REQUIREMENTS:

    40 cm x 35 cm (16" x 14") piece of silk, satin or a fabric of your choice

    A lace motif of your choice. These motifs are readily available at craft and haberdashery shops.

THREADS REQUIRED:

    DCM stranded cotton (floss)

Blanc neige, white	502 blue green
209 lavender, dark	963 dusty rose, ultra light
211 lavender, light	3687 mauve
340 blue violet	3688 mauve, medium
341 blue violet, light	3689 mauve, light
407 sportsman flesh, dark	lemon of your choice
501 blue green, dark	

Actual size

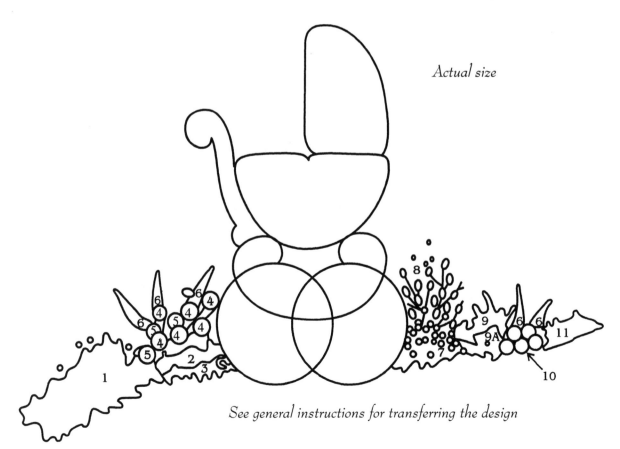

See general instructions for transferring the design

ADDITIONAL REQUIREMENTS:

An embroidery hoop

A variety of needles of various sizes

METHOD:

Stitch the lace motif in position.

Using a soft lead pencil, gently outline the shape of the flowers.

1. Using three strands of blanc neige, together with one strand of 407, work 50–60 knots, scattering them through the area. Using six strands of blanc neige work about 30 knots scattered through those already worked.

With three strands of 502, fill remaining unworked spaces with an occasional knot scattered outside the white knots.

2. Using two strands of 209, together with one strand of 211, fill most of the area with knots. Then using three strands of 211, fill any remaining spaces. Using two strands of 209, scatter a few knots on top of those already worked.

3. Using two strands of 501, fill the area.

4. Using one strand of 3688, together with one strand of 3689, fill the areas.

With two strands of 3689, work several knots over the area already worked.

5. Using two strands of 3689 fill the areas and using two strands of 502, fill the area between 2 and 4.

6. Using two strands of 340, fill with knots.

7. Using six strands of 963, fill the upper section of this area with knots and then using two strands of 502, fill the lower section of this area with knots.

8. Using two strands of 341, work scattered clusters of three knots then, using two strands of 340, work two knots at the base of the clusters already worked. Scatter an odd single knot at the top of this area.

Take a single strand of 501 and work some straight stitches to represent stems between these flowers.

9. With two strands of 3689 together with one strand of 3687, fill most of the upper section with knots. Then with three strands of 3689, fill remaining unworked

areas between the knots already worked.

9a. Using two strands of 501, fill lower section with knots.

10. Work five flowers. Using three strands of lemon, work one knot in the centre of each flower. Using three strands of blanc neige, work five or six knots around each lemon centre.

11. Using two strands of 3689, fill most of the area with knots. Then using two strands of 501, scatter knots between the lower section of the pink knots.

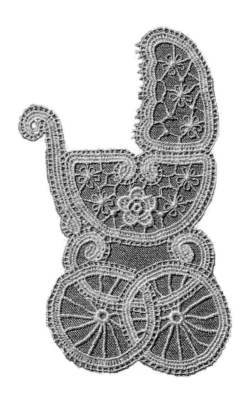

The Pergola

This picture is larger than the size usually recommended but it is well worth the effort.

FABRIC REQUIRED:

> 30 cm (12") square piece of silk, satin, taffeta, or fabric of your choice.

THREADS REQUIRED:

DMC stranded cotton (floss)

Blanc neige, white	841 beige brown, light
ecru	842 beige brown, very light
209 lavender, dark	928 grey green, very light
309 rose, deep	3012 khaki green, medium
335 rose	3013 khaki green, light
341 blue violet, light	3041 antique violet, medium
605 cranberry, very light	3042 antique violet, light
712 cream	3328 salmon, dark
726 topaz, light	3363 pine green, medium
745 yellow, light pale	3364 pine green
746 off white	3688 mauve, medium
760 salmon	3689 mauve, light
761 salmon, light	3713 salmon, very light
776 pink, medium	3731 dusty rose, very dark
783 topaz, medium	3743 antique violet, very light
818 baby pink	3746 blue violet, dark
839 beige brown, dark	3756 baby blue, very light
840 beige brown, medium	

50 cm (½yd) x 2 mm (1/16") very bright salmon-pink silk ribbon
50 cm (½yd) x 2 mm (1/16") shell-pink silk ribbon
30 cm (12") x 2 mm (1/16") mauve-pink silk ribbon to tone with DMC 3688 and 3689

ADDITIONAL REQUIREMENTS:

> An embroidery hoop
> A variety of needles of various sizes, including a crewel needle

Actual size

See general instructions for transferring the design

METHOD:

1. Using six strands of 726 together with one strand of 783, fill approximately half the area.
   Then using three strands of 726 together with one strand of 783, fill in most of the remaining area, leaving a little room for greenery. These knots should be concentrated in the upper and middle areas of this section. Using one strand of 3363 together with one strand of 3364, fill any unworked spaces.

2. Using three strands of 341 together with three strands of 3746, fill most of the area. With two strands of 3364, fill any unworked spaces.

3. With two strands of 3688 together with two strands of 3689, scatter clusters of three knots throughout the

area. Using two strands of 3688, work a few more knots over each cluster.

Using two strands of 928, fill any unworked area.

Using a single strand of 3364, scatter some knots throughout the area.

4. Using three strands of 760 together with three strands of 3328, fill most of the area.

   With three strands of 3363, fill remaining unworked area. Towards the outer edge of this area do not work the knots closely together, but scatter a few at random.

5. Using the following combination – three strands of 746, two strands of 760, together with one strand of 3328, scatter knots through the area.

   With one strand of 928 together with one strand of 3364, work knots closely together on the right-hand side of this section (that is, the end that joins section 1). As you work away from this end of the section, scatter knots so that they become quite sparse.

6. Using two strands of 341 together with one strand of 761, fill the area. Work a few extra knots on top of the base layer of knots.

   Using two strands of 3364, fill a few small spaces on the sides of these flowers.

7. With two strands of 761 together with one strand of 3713, fill the area and then work a few extra knots on top of the base layer of knots.

   Using two strands of 3364, fill a few small spaces on the sides of the flowers.

8. Take two strands of 746 together with two strands of 3328 and work clusters of six to eight knots.

   Using one strand of 3013 together with one strand of 3012, fill the remaining area.

   Using a single strand of 3013, work some vertical straight stitches on top of the green knots to represent stems.

9. Using five strands of 746 together with one strand of 783, work the knots closely together at the top of the area, scattering them more sparsely as you work toward the bottom of the area.

   Using one strand of 3363 together with one strand of

3364, once again work most of the knots at the top of the area (between those already worked), scattering them more sparsely as you work towards the bottom of the area.

10. Take the bright salmon-pink silk ribbon and work knots closely together.

Using this same silk ribbon, scatter about five knots through and on the edge of section 4.

Using two strands of 3363, fill the unworked area.

10a. Work as for 10, using shell-pink silk ribbon.

11. With four strands of 209 together with two strands of 605, fill most of the area but scattering some of the knots on the right-hand side of the area quite sparsely.

12. Using two strands of 746 together with one strand of 309, scatter clusters of knots so that approximately half the area is filled. Then, taking two strands of 3364, fill the unworked area.

13. Using two strands of 3756, fill almost all of the area and then with one strand of 3364, fill the remaining small gaps.

14. Use two strands of 209 to fill the area and with a single strand of 3364, work an occasional knot through the area.

15. Using one strand of 746 together with one strand of 761, fill the area.

Using a single strand of 3364, work an occasional knot through the area.

16. With a single strand of 3756, fill most of the area and then use two strands of 341 to fill the remaining spaces.

The Pergola:

A. Using two strands of 842, work a few vertical rows consisting of three to five knots.

Using two strands of 841, work a few more vertical rows consisting of three to five knots.

With one strand of 841 together with one strand of 842, fill the remaining area.

B. & C. Using a single strand of 840, fill the area.

D. Using two strands of 840, fill the area.

With a single strand of 839, work a single row of

knots along the length of the lower edge of D, keeping these knots very close to those already worked.

E. Using a single strand of 839, fill the area.

F. Using two strands of 842, work several rows of knots the length of the post. Leave a small area in the centre of the post unworked. This area will be filled with flowers later.

Still leaving the small area in the centre of the post unworked, fill any remaining unworked areas of the post with two strands of 841.

Using a single strand of 839, work about five to six vertical short straight stitches on top of the knots on A, B, C, D and E.

G. Using a single strand of 839, fill the area.

Still using a single strand of 839, work single rows of knots where indicated by the lines between the areas marked G.

Using a single strand of 3041, fill about half of the area between the areas marked G.

Using a single strand of 3042, fill most of the remaining area between the areas marked G.

Using a single strand of 3012, fill any remaining spaces in this section.

17. With a single strand of 745 fill most of the area and then use a single strand of 3364 to fill the remaining area.

18. Using a single strand of 341, fill the area, clustering the knots very closely together. Work a few extra knots on top of those already worked.

18a Using a single strand of 761, fill the area.

18b Using a single strand of 309, fill the area.

19. Using the mauve-pink silk ribbon and a No 8 crewel needle, cluster the knots closely together. Pull the knots tightly so that they are small.

20. Using two strands of 746, fill the area.

Using a single strand of 746, scatter an occasional knot just above sections 16, 17 and 18 so that you have flowers at different heights.

21. Using a single strand of 3012, cluster small groups of knots together so that at least half of this area is covered.

Using a single strand of 3042, scatter small clusters of

knots between those already worked.

With a single strand of 3013, fill any remaining spaces.

Using a single strand of 818, scatter a few knots on top of those already worked.

22. With a single strand of 3042, fill the upper left-hand corner of this section and then scatter knots through the remaining area.

    Using a single strand of 3013, fill half the remaining area, then use a single strand of 3012 to fill any remaining unworked area.

23. Using a single strand of 746, fill the area.

24. Using a single strand of 309, fill the area.

25. Using a single strand of 745, fill the area, clustering the knots very closely together and then working a few extra knots on top of the base layer.

    Using a single strand of 3364, scatter a few green knots through sections 23, 24 and 25.

26. With a single strand of 746, fill the areas. Work a second layer of knots over the base layer only over the lower half of these flowers. This will help achieve a three-dimensional appearance.

    The arch under the pergola: With a single strand of 3012, outline the arch and then scatter a few knots just above the line already worked. Using a single strand of 335, scatter knots just above the outline and through the green knots already worked. **Do not** work either of these colours **under** the arch.

    Using a single strand of 818, fill any small gaps that remain, forming the arch area.

    Using a single strand of 335 and then 818, work a few knots on top of those already worked. When finished the arch will be approximately 3 mm (⅛") wide.

27. Begin at the upper left-hand corner. Using a single strand of 3042 then 3013, scatter an equal number of knots of each colour, leaving a few small spaces unworked.

    Using two strands of 818, work knots in these small unworked spaces. Also, work about three knots in the upper right-hand corner of section 22 on top of those already worked.

Move across to the right-hand side of this section and, using a single strand of 3041, fill approximately half of the area.

Using a single strand each of 3042, 3012 and 3013, fill all of the remaining spaces in this section.

28. Using three strands of blanc neige together with one strand of 3013, fill most of the area.

    Using two strands of 3012, fill the remaining spaces.

29. Using a single strand of 3012, work clusters of knots on the right-hand side of this section and then scatter knots through the remaining area.

    Using a single strand of 3042, work small clusters of knots through the area.

    Using a single strand of 3013, fill in any remaining spaces.

30. Using a single strand of 3042, work a single row of knots across the bottom of this section to define the area.

    With a single strand of 3743 and then 712, fill with equal numbers of each colour.

    The path: The knots forming the path should not be worked as closely together as the rest of the embroidery. As you work towards the bottom of the picture, the density of the knots will decrease so that they become quite sparse at the lower edge.

31. Using a single strand of 3042, work some broken horizontal lines of this colour through the area.

    Using a single strand of 842, work more broken horizontal lines.

    Using a single strand of 712, fill any remaining unworked spaces.

32. Using a single strand of 842, work the areas at the edge of the path, close to the flowers where indicated by the shading. Scatter an occasional knot of this colour through the area.

    Using a single strand of 712, fill the remaining area.

    Note: In the areas 33 and 34, the knots are very heavily massed together with additional knots worked on top of the base layer. Towards the outer edge of the section the knots are very sparse and scattered.

33. With two strands and then four strands of ecru, scatter

knots throughout the area.

Using two strands and then four strands of 818, scatter knots throughout the area.

Using one strand of 776 together with one strand of 818, and then two strands of each colour worked together, scatter more knots.

The greenery: Using 3012 and 3013 and using one, two and three strands in varying colour combinations, fill any unworked areas. Then using the pinks and ecru, work additional knots on top of the base layer.

34. Work as for 33 using the following combinations:

Two and four strands of 3713.

Two strands of 3713, together with two strands of 3731.

One strand of 3713 together with one strand of 3731.

The greenery is as 33, once again working additional pink knots on top of the base layer.

The high area in the centre of this section is worked with scattered single-strand 3012.

Remember to fill the unworked area of pergola post F with pink knots.

The Blossom Tree

Whenever I teach classes, scenes featuring blossom trees are always very popular. This scene has been worked by many of my students.

FABRIC REQUIRED:

> 20 cm (8") square piece of calico

THREAD REQUIRED:

> DMC stranded cotton (floss)

Blanc neige, white	745 yellow, light pale
ecru	819 baby pink, light
210 lavender, medium	3011 khaki green, dark
301 mahogany, medium	3012 khaki green, medium
340 blue violet, medium	3013 khaki green, light
341 blue violet, light	3042 antique violet, light
407 sportsman flesh, dark	3047 yellow beige, light
420 hazelnut brown, dark	3053 green grey
422 hazelnut brown, light	3348 yellow green, light
524 fern green, very light	3364 pine green
676 old gold, light	3688 mauve, medium
677 old gold, very light	3689 mauve, light
726 topaz, light	3727 antique mauve, light
733 olive green, medium	3743 antique violet, very light
734 olive green, light	3747 blue violet, very light
738 tan, very light	3772 negro flesh
739 tan, ultra very light	
744 yellow, pale	

ADDITIONAL REQUIREMENTS:

> 30 cm x 2 mm (12" x 1/16") very bright pink silk ribbon
> A small embroidery hoop
> A variety of needles

METHOD:

1. Using one strand of 340 together with one strand of 341, fill the areas, massing the knots very closely together.

   Using a single strand of 3727, work some knots between those already worked. Introduce this colour on the left-hand side of the picture so that this colour is

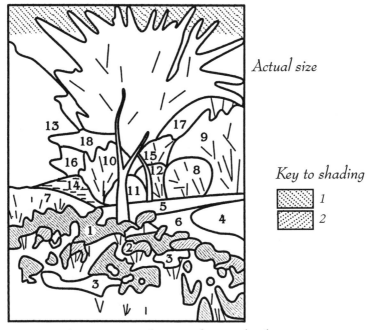

Actual size

Key to shading

▨	*1*
▨	*2*

See general instructions for transferring the design

quite dense on the left but decreasing to nothing around the centre of the picture.

With a single strand of 3747, scatter knots through those already worked.

2. Using one strand of 744 together with one strand of 745, fill the areas, massing the knots very closely together.

3. With four strands of blanc neige together with one strand of 726, fill the area on the right-hand side. For the second and larger area, scatter about 15 knots. The remaining unworked area will be filled with grass.

Using four strands of 726, scatter about 20 knots across the lower half of the section already worked.

The grass between sections 1, 2 and 3:
Begin in the lower right-hand corner.

Using a single strand of 3743, work the knots so that about half the area is filled with this colour. The number of knots of this colour should decrease as you work towards the centre of the picture. If you wish to work your initials and the date, do so at this point in the lower left-hand corner in a colour of your choice.

With a single strand of 3743, scatter small clusters of

knots on the right-hand side of the picture.

Using a single strand of 3012, work two or three knots under each yellow flower.

Using a single strand of 3364, concentrate quite a few knots of this colour in the centre of this area and up towards the top of the left-hand side.

Using a single strand of 3013, fill any remaining unworked areas.

Using a single strand of 3012, work some vertical straight stitches scattered through the area.

4. Using a single strand of 3364, work a broken line of knots around the edge of this section and then scatter about 15 knots over half this area (the half nearest the path).

With one strand of 340 together with one strand of 341, work a cluster of 10 knots on the top right-hand side.

Using a single strand of 3747, scatter about 15 knots through the area.

Using a single strand of 3743, scatter about 20 knots through the area.

Using a single strand of 3013, fill the remaining area.

The tree trunks:

Work the largest tree first.

With a single strand of 420, work the outline of the trunk. Work several small clusters of knots in the trunk. As you work up the trunk, the knots will decrease in number, gradually trailing off to nothing.

Using a single strand of 422, fill the unworked areas of the trunk.

Using a single strand of 420, work a few extra knots on top of those already worked on the trunk.

The smaller tree: Using a single strand of 420, work knots on the left-hand side of the trunk to mark the outline.

Using a single strand of 422, work a few knots on the right-hand side of the trunk. Then for both trees, use a single strand of 420 and scatter some straight stitches for the upper fine branches.

5. Using a single strand of 3364, work a solid line of knots along the line which separates 5 from 6. Scatter

a few knots close to this line inside this area.

With a single strand of 340, work a broken, uneven line across the top of this area.

Using a single strand of 3743, fill about half of the remaining area, and then using a single strand of 3013, fill any remaining unworked spaces.

6. Using a single strand of 738 fill most of the area. With a single strand of 739, fill any remaining unworked spaces.

7. Using a single strand of 340, work knots closely together across the top of this section.

   Using a single strand of 3042, work more knots between those already worked and scatter quite a few of this colour throughout the area.

   Using a single strand of 3012, fill approximately half the remaining area and using a single strand of 3364, fill any remaining unworked spaces. Still using this colour, work short straight vertical stitches scattered over the area.

   Using the very bright pink silk ribbon, scatter about 12 knots through the grassed areas already worked.

8. Using one strand of 733 together with one strand of 734, fill approximately half the area with knots.

   Using two strands of blanc neige, scatter knots throughout the area.

   Using a single strand of 420, fill any remaining small spaces and then work some straight stitches over the knots.

9. Using one strand of 210 together with one strand of 3727, fill most of the top section of this area. As you work from the top of the section towards the bottom, decrease the number of knots.

   Using one strand of 3053 together with one strand of 3348, fill about half the remaining area with knots.

   Using a single strand of 3013, fill about half the remaining area with knots.

   Using a single strand 3047, fill any remaining unworked spaces.

   Using a single strand of 3012, work some straight stitches on top of the knots.

10. Using one strand of 733 together with one strand of

734, scatter about 18 knots through the area.

Using two strands of blanc neige scatter about 15 knots through the area.

Using a single strand of 733, scatter knots through the area and use a single strand of 3013 to fill any remaining unworked spaces.

Using a single strand of 3011, work a few straight stitches on top of the knots.

11. Using a single strand of 3011, fill approximately half the area with knots.

    With a single strand of 3012, fill approximately half of the remaining area and use a single strand of 3727 to fill any remaining small spaces.

12. Using a single strand of 3727, scatter about eight knots through the top half of this area.

    Using a single strand of 210, fill the remaining top section of this area and also scatter several knots in the lower half.

    Using a single strand of 3348, fill half the remaining area with knots.

    With a single strand of 3053, fill any small spaces and then work a few short straight stitches on top of the knots.

13. Using three strands of blanc neige, scatter approximately 40 knots through this area. Some of these knots will be single knots, but also work some clusters of two or three knots.

    Using two strands of 819, work some knots around those already worked and scatter an occasional single knot through the area.

    Using one strand of blanc neige together with one strand of 819, scatter knots so that about half the area is filled.

    Using a single strand of 676, scatter some knots through the area.

    Using a single strand of 3047, scatter an equal number of knots of this colour.

    Using a single strand of 3042, scatter some knots through the area. Using a single strand of 3743, fill any remaining small spaces.

14. With a single strand of 3727, scatter a few knots through the area.

Using a single strand of 3747, fill the remaining area then work a few small straight horizontal stitches over the knots.

The blossom tree: With two strands of 3689 together with one strand of 3688, scatter approximately 100 knots through the tree area, concentrating most of the knots along the branches, with occasional clusters between the branches.

Using one strand of 819 together with one strand of 3689, work knots around those already worked so that about half the total area is filled.

Using a single strand of 819, work some more knots around the clusters already worked. As you get to the outer ends of the branches decrease the numbers of knots so that they are trailing off to nothing.

Using a single strand of 734, work a few knots through the tree area and then use a single strand of 677 to work some more knots through the tree area.

With a single strand of blanc neige, work knots on top of and through the pink knots already worked. You may still have some spaces between the branches of blossom which will be filled with blue when the sky is worked.

15. Using a single strand of 407, fill about half of the area. Using a single strand of 3772, fill approximately half the remaining area. Using a single strand of 301, fill any remaining small spaces. Work a few short straight stitches on top of the knots.

16. Using a single strand of each of the following colours, 524, 3743 and 745, fill the area with an equal number of knots of each colour.

17. Using a single strand of 3053, work 10–12 knots scattered through the area. The remaining unworked spaces will be filled when the sky is worked.

18. Using a single strand of 3743, scatter several knots through the area.

Using a single strand of 3053, scatter several knots through the area. The remaining unworked area will be filled when the sky is being worked.

The sky: For the shaded area at the top of the picture, use a single strand of 341 to scatter knots across this area.

Using a single strand of ecru, scatter an equal number of knots across this area, and then use a single strand of 3747 to fill all of the remaining spaces, including those left in 17 and 18.

Lingerie Bag

Lingerie bags are always popular. This simple design would make an ideal gift.

FABRIC REQUIRED:

> 96 cm x 30 cm (38" x 12") moiré taffeta, or fabric of your choice

THREADS REQUIRED:

> DMC stranded cotton (floss)
> 745 yellow, light pale
> 799 delft, medium
> 991 aquamarine, dark
> 3326 rose, light

ADDITIONAL REQUIREMENTS:

> Small embroidery hoop
> 8 crewel, straw or milliner's needle.
> 1 m x 5 mm (1 yd x ¼") satin ribbon to match the fabric

Actual size

745 and 799

} 3326

° French knot

⌒ Lazy daisy

\ Straight stitch

See general instructions for transferring design

METHOD:

> Fold the fabric in half so that the short sides are together. Press along the fold. Begin the embroidery with the large spray, the lower edge of which will be about 12 cm (5") from the fold.
> Using three strands of 745, work the flower centres.
> Using three strands of 799, work five knots around each centre.
> With two strands of 991, work the straight stitches,

the lazy daisy leaves and the small French knots.

Using three strands of 3326, work the pink knots. Scatter the smaller sprays at random working the smaller sprays in the same way as the large spray.

With right sides together, join the side seams. Hem the top of the bag.

Using a buttonhole stitch, work keepers on both sides of the bag 8 cm (3¼") from the top. Thread the ribbon through the keepers.

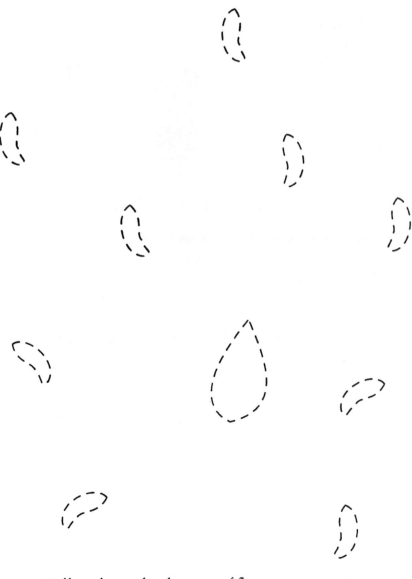

Half-size layout for placement of flowers

Pot Pourri Stem

FABRIC REQUIREMENTS:

42 cm x 35 cm (16½" x 1¼") wide taffeta or satin ribbon

20 cm (8") x 2 mm (1/16") silk or satin ribbon to match

THREADS REQUIRED:

DMC stranded cotton (floss)

ecru

368 pistachio green, light

745 yellow, pale light

809 delft

3341 apricot

745 , ecru and 3341

809

3341

368

METHOD:

See general instructions for transferring the design

Using three strands of 745, work the flower centres.

Using three strands ecru, work five knots around three of the flower centres.

Using three strands of 3341, work five knots around the remaining three flower centres.

Using three strands of 809, scatter clusters of three knots through the spray.

Using two strands of 3341 then 368, scatter occasional knots through the spray.

Using two strands of 368, work some straight stitch stems.

Using a single strand of either ecru or 3341, couch a small bow at the base of the spray.

Fold the ribbon in half and fold the ends in about 2–2.5 cm (1").

Slip stitch the sides of the ribbon together.

Fill the stem with lavender or pot pourri.

Tie the bag with the silk or satin ribbon.

Vase of Flowers

While recovering from an accident last year, a friend presented me with a beautiful bunch of delphiniums. The colours really appealed to me, so I embroidered the arrangement. This spray could be used on a number of small projects, for example, a pot pourri bag, framed picture, paperweight or, as I have done, the lid of a porcelain box. I have used a few lazy daisy stitches for leaves.

FABRIC REQUIRED:

A small piece, maximum size 20 cm x 20 cm (8" x 8") of fabric of your choice; silk, satin or taffeta would be suitable.

THREADS REQUIRED:

For vase: Waterlilies by Caron 12 ply silk, colour: Morning Mist, or stranded cotton or silk in the colour of your choice

Blanc neige, white	605 cranberry, very light
209 lavender	961 dusty rose
340 blue violet	963 dusty rose, dark
341 blue violet, light	3364 pine green
522 fern green	3689 mauve, light
604 cranberry, light	3727 antique mauve, light

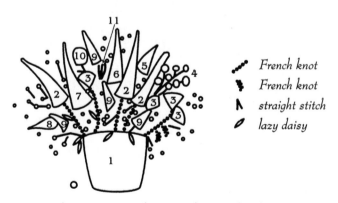

● French knot	
❧ French knot	
Λ straight stitch	
⊘ lazy daisy	

See general instructions for transferring the design

METHOD:

Using a soft lead pencil, lightly outline the vase and flowers, 2–11.

1. *Vase:* Fill the entire area with knots using a single strand of silk or cotton.

2. *Larkspurs:* This flower is worked with two strands of 963. Fill the area with knots. Work another four to

six knots on top of the knots already worked in the lower section of the flower. This will give the flower a rounded, more natural appearance.

3. *Trumpet flowers:* These flowers are worked with a single strand. Stems: Using 522, work a row of knots.
   Leaves: Work five knots in an arc, then two or three knots in the centre of the arc.
   Outline the sides of the flower with 605. Fill the area with 3689.
   Using 604 and beginning at the base of the flower, work three small straight stitches over the knots the full length of the flower. One stitch on each side and one stitch down the centre of the flower.

4. *Statice:* This flower is worked with a single strand.
   Stems: Using 522, work straight stitches.
   Flowers: Using 209, work small clusters of knots.
   All Delphiniums:
   Stems and leaves are worked with a single strand of 522.
   Stems are knots. Leaves are a small lazy daisy.

5. *Delphiniums:* Using a single strand of 340, fill the area with knots.
   Delphiniums 6, 7, 8 and 9 are all worked with two strands.

6. *Delphinium:* Using one strand of 340 together with one strand of 3727, fill the area with knots.

7. *Delphinium:* Using 340, fill the lower half of the area with knots.
   Then using one strand of 340 together with one strand of 3727, fill the remaining top portion of the flower.

8. *Delphinium:* Using 341, fill the area with knots.

9. *Delphinium:* Using one strand of blanc neige together with one strand of 3364, fill the area with knots.

10. *Dahlia:* Using three strands of 961, work four knots closely together. Then using a single strand of the same colour, work a circle of knots around these larger central knots.

11. *Bullion rose bud:* Using a single strand of 3727, work three bullion stitches of eight wraps side by side.

Baby's breath: This flower is represented on the illustration by small circles and straight lines. It surrounds the main spray. Using a single strand of 522, work some straight stitches and a few scattered knots.

Using two strands of blanc neige, work some scattered knots. Some of these white knots should sit directly above the knots already worked in green. The green represents the calyx. Scatter additional white knots to fill in some of the gaps.

Brooch

This is a small project that can be completed quickly — within about one hour. It would make an ideal gift.

THREADS REQUIRED:

> DMC stranded cotton (floss)
> 341 blue violet, light
> 743 yellow, medium
> 745 yellow, pale light
> 3687 mauve
> 3688 mauve, medium
> 3713 salmon, very light

ADDITIONAL REQUIREMENTS:

> small embroidery hoop
> small oval brooch (available from most craft shops and the larger department stores)
> No 10 or No 9 crewel needle
> 10 cm (4") square piece of silk, taffeta, or fabric of your choice

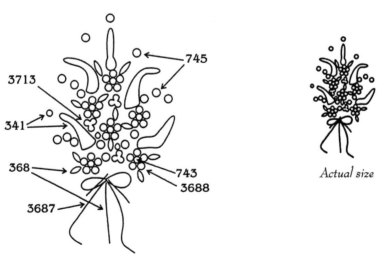

Actual size

See general instructions for transferring the design

METHOD:

> Using the back of the brooch as a template, draw a pencil line in the shape of the oval, in the centre of your fabric.
> Work the design as follows:
> Using two strands of 743, work one knot for the centre

of each mauve flower.

Using two strands of 3688, work five knots around each yellow centre. Work these knots close to the centre knot.

With a single strand of 341, work the small sprays of knots. These knots are massed together at the base of the sprays.

Using a single strand of 368, work very small lazy daisy leaves and the stems.

Using two strands of 3713, work clusters of three knots scattered through the spray.

Using two strands of 745, work sprays of knots and fill any small spaces that may remain in the centre of the spray with a single knot.

Using a single strand of 3687, couch a small bow at the base of the spray.

Complete the brooch following the assembly instructions given with the brooch.